Share Your Stories

ISBN 13: 978-1-55517-960-6 (Grandma)
ISBN 10: 1-55517-960-6 (Grandma)
ISBN 13: 978-1-55517-958-4 (Mother)
ISBN 10: 1-55517-958-4 (Mother)

Published by CFI, an imprint of Cedar Fort, Inc.
925 N. Main, Springville, UT, 84663
Distributed by Cedar Fort, Inc. www.cedarfort.com

Cover design by Nicole Williams
Cover design © 2006 by Lyle Mortimer
Printed in the United States of America

10 9 8 7 6 5 4 3 2 1

Printed on acid-free paper

The Importance of Writing Your Life Story

Why should you write your life story? If you don't do it, no one else will. No one else can! No one else knows the experiences and lessons of your life. If you don't write about your life, then the only thing people will know about you is the dash between your birth date and your death date. You have so much to offer. You are unique.

Consider these insightful statements by general authorities:

President Spencer W. Kimball

"I urge all of the people of this church to give serious attention to their family histories, to encourage their parents and grandparents to write their journals, and let no family go into eternity without having left their memoirs for their children, their grandchildren, and their posterity. This is a duty and a responsibility, and I urge every person to start the children out writing a personal history and journal" ("The True Way of Life and Salvation," *Ensign*, May 1978, 4).

"I promise you that if you will keep your journals and records, they will indeed be a source of great inspiration to your families . . . and others, on through the generations. . . . And as our posterity read of our life's experiences, they, too, will come to know and love us. And in that glorious day when our families are together in the eternities, we will already be acquainted. . . .

"Your journal is your autobiography, so it should be kept carefully. You are unique, and there may be incidents in your experience that are more noble and praiseworthy in their way than those recorded in any other life" ("President Kimball Speaks Out on Personal Journals," *New Era*, December 1980, 26–27).

"People often use the excuse that their lives are uneventful and nobody would be interested in what they have done. But I promise you that if you will keep your journals and records they will indeed be a source of great inspiration to your families, to your children, your grandchildren, and others, on through the generations" ("Hold Fast to the Iron Rod," *Ensign,* October 1978, 4).

Elder Theodore M. Burton

"Not everything we do is important. Not everything we write is important. Not everything we think is important. But occasionally we are in tune with God. . . . When we write by the Spirit and they read by the Spirit, there is a godly communication between us and them which makes that which we write become meaningful and a source of inspiration to our descendants" (Theodore M. Burton, "The Inspiration of a Family Record," *Ensign,* Jan. 1977, 17).

It's Easy to Write Your Personal History

To write your personal life story, simply read and write answers to the questions in each section that follows. Don't try to write your entire history all at once. Just take it one section at a time. When you begin to write, imagine that you are talking to your loved ones across a kitchen table. Simply answer the questions (out loud, if it helps), and then write down those thoughts and feelings as if you were speaking to your immediate family face-to-face.

Here's a simple suggestion to begin writing your life story. Each week, try writing one page, or even just a single paragraph, about yourself by responding to the questions that follow. At the end of one year, you will have fifty-two paragraphs, pages, or stories—personal memories recorded for your children and grandchildren to treasure. Smile for your posterity by including photographs for each section you write.

Remember, if you don't tell your story, no one else will. You are unique, and your posterity will come to know and love you as they read your story in the only words that can properly tell it: your own.

Childhood

(Birth to 11 years old)

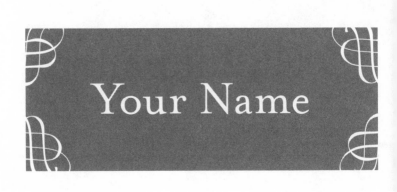

Your Name

What is your full name?

YOUR NAME

2

Why were you given your name? Were you
named after someone else?

_____

_____

_____

_____

_____

_____

_____

_____

_____

_____

_____

_____

_____

_____

_____

_____

_____

_____

_____

_____

_____

Did you have a nickname as you were growing up? What was it, and how did you get it? Have you had any other nicknames during your life?

_____
_____
_____
_____
_____
_____
_____
_____
_____
_____
_____
_____
_____
_____
_____
_____
_____

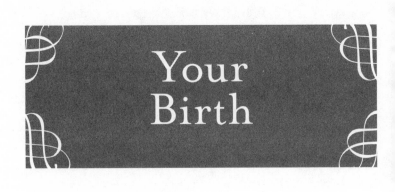

Your
Birth

When and where were you born? What
was your weight and length? How tall
are you now?

_____
_____
_____
_____
_____
_____
_____
_____
_____
_____
_____
_____
_____
_____
_____
_____
_____
_____
_____

2

What color was your hair when you were born?

3

Were there any unusual circumstances surrounding your birth?

4

Who was president of the United States
when you were born? Who was the
president of the Church?

_____

_____

_____

_____

_____

_____

_____

_____

_____

_____

_____

_____

_____

_____

_____

_____

_____

_____

_____

_____

Your
Family

1

From which countries did your ancestors emigrate? How did they travel? When did they arrive? Where did they settle?

_____

_____

_____

_____

_____

_____

_____

_____

_____

_____

_____

_____

_____

_____

_____

_____

_____

_____

_____

_____

Who are your parents? What are their full
names? Where and when were they born?
Where did they grow up?

What did your parents do for a living?

4

What do you remember most about your
father from your childhood? About your
mother?

_____
_____
_____
_____
_____
_____
_____
_____
_____
_____
_____
_____
_____
_____
_____
_____
_____
_____
_____
_____
_____

5

Who were your grandparents? What do
you remember about each of them? How
old were you when your grandparents
died?

_____

_____

_____

_____

_____

_____

_____

_____

_____

_____

_____

_____

_____

_____

_____

_____

_____

_____

_____

6

Who is the oldest person in your family
you can remember knowing when you were
a child? What do you remember about that
person?

_____

_____

_____

_____

_____

_____

_____

_____

_____

_____

_____

_____

_____

_____

_____

_____

_____

7

While you were growing up, which languages were spoken in your home?

8

What are the full names of your brothers
and sisters? Where was your family living
when they were born?

_____

_____

_____

_____

_____

_____

_____

_____

_____

_____

_____

_____

_____

_____

_____

_____

_____

_____

_____

_____

9

Share a memory of your brothers and sisters. To whom did you feel closest? Why?

_____
_____
_____
_____
_____
_____
_____
_____
_____
_____
_____
_____
_____
_____
_____
_____
_____
_____
_____
_____

10

Where was your first home? What are your earliest memories of your home? Can you draw a floor plan of your home?

_____

_____

_____

_____

_____

_____

_____

_____

_____

_____

_____

_____

_____

_____

_____

_____

_____

_____

11

What was the yard like?

12

What was your room like?

13

What was your favorite thing in the house or yard?

14

Where has your family lived since that time?

15

What did your family do for fun when you were a child?

16

What did you talk about at dinner?

17

How did your family spend time together?

_____

_____

_____

_____

_____

_____

_____

_____

_____

_____

_____

_____

_____

_____

_____

_____

_____

_____

_____

_____

_____

_____

18

Was there a chore you hated doing as a child?

19

What appliances did you have (or not have) in your home?

20

Did you have any favorite uncles, aunts, or cousins growing up? Who were they, and what did you admire most about them?

_____

_____

_____

_____

_____

_____

_____

_____

_____

_____

_____

_____

_____

_____

_____

_____

_____

_____

21

Where did your family go on vacation?
What are your favorite memories of the
trips you took together?

_____

_____

_____

_____

_____

_____

_____

_____

_____

_____

_____

_____

_____

_____

_____

_____

_____

_____

_____

Your Childhood

As a young child, what did you look like?

_____

_____

_____

_____

_____

_____

_____

_____

_____

_____

_____

_____

_____

_____

_____

_____

_____

_____

_____

_____

SHARE YOUR STORIES

2

What is the earliest thing you remember?

3

Who were your best friends in your early
years? Did you ever have sleepovers?

4

What kinds of things did you like to do? What were your favorite childhood games to play?

5

Do you remember having a favorite
nursery rhyme or bedtime story? What
kinds of books did you like to read?

_____
_____
_____
_____
_____
_____
_____
_____
_____
_____
_____
_____
_____
_____
_____
_____
_____
_____
_____
_____
_____

6

Who pulled your teeth when they were
loose? How was it done? How much did
the tooth fairy leave for a lost tooth?

_____

_____

_____

_____

_____

_____

_____

_____

_____

_____

_____

_____

_____

_____

_____

_____

_____

7

What was the climate of the area where you grew up?

8

What was your favorite toy?

9

How many pets did you have? Which one was your favorite pet?

10

What were your pets like? Do you have a
favorite story about one of your pets?

11

Did you have any childhood diseases or health problems? Any stitches or broken bones?

_____

_____

_____

_____

_____

_____

_____

_____

_____

_____

_____

_____

_____

_____

_____

_____

_____

_____

_____

12

Have you ever been hospitalized, or have
you had surgery? What for?

13

What were some of the best experiences in your early life?

_____

_____

_____

_____

_____

_____

_____

_____

_____

_____

_____

_____

_____

_____

_____

_____

_____

_____

_____

_____

_____

_____

...(continued)

14

Do you remember how much things like gasoline, stamps, and food cost? During what years were these prices valid?

_____

_____

_____

_____

_____

_____

_____

_____

_____

_____

_____

_____

_____

_____

_____

_____

_____

_____

_____

_____

15

What were your favorite family traditions?

16

Do you have any special memories of holidays or family reunions?

17

What did you do on Valentine's Day? Did you make your own valentines? How did you deliver them? Did you have a valentine box at school?

18

What did you do on Easter? Did you dye
eggs and hide baskets?

19

What did you do on the Fourth of July?
Did you set off your own fireworks? Did
you have a barbecue or picnic?

20

What did you do on Halloween? What did you wear for costumes? Did you make your own costumes or buy them from the store?

_____

_____

_____

_____

_____

_____

_____

_____

_____

_____

_____

_____

_____

_____

_____

_____

_____

_____

_____

21

On Halloween, did you play tricks on anyone, or visa versa? Did you go trick-or-treating?

22

What did you do on Thanksgiving? Who came to visit? Where did you go to eat?

23

What did you do on Christmas? Did Santa visit your home? Did you ever see or talk to him? Did you hang stockings? What did Santa leave in them?

_____

_____

_____

_____

_____

_____

_____

_____

_____

_____

_____

_____

_____

_____

_____

_____

_____

_____

24

On Christmas, what time did you get up in the morning?

25

Did you have a Christmas tree? Buy it? Cut it? What were the decorations like? Tell about your most memorable Christmas.

_____

_____

_____

_____

_____

_____

_____

_____

_____

_____

_____

_____

_____

_____

_____

_____

_____

_____

26

What did you do on New Year's Eve? Were you allowed to stay up until midnight? Did you do anything special at midnight?

_____

_____

_____

_____

_____

_____

_____

_____

_____

_____

_____

_____

_____

_____

_____

_____

_____

_____

27

How is the world different now from what
it was like when you were a child?

Adolescence
(11 to 18 years old)

Schooling

1

Where did you go to elementary or grade school? Who were your teachers?

2

What was your school like? How did you get to school?

_____

_____

_____

_____

_____

_____

_____

_____

_____

_____

_____

_____

_____

_____

_____

_____

_____

_____

_____

_____

_____

_____

3

What memories do you have from elementary school?

4

What did you do at recess? What games did you play?

_____

_____

_____

_____

_____

_____

_____

_____

_____

_____

_____

_____

_____

_____

_____

_____

_____

_____

_____

_____

5

Did you ever skip school?

6

What subjects or programs do you remember?

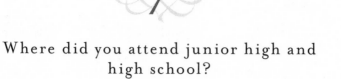

7

Where did you attend junior high and high school?

8

How did you like school?

9

What was your favorite subject? Why?

10

Who were your favorite teachers? Why were they special to you?

11

Who were your friends during junior high and high school? Did you and your friends have a special hangout where you liked to spend time? Where was it, and what did you do there?

_____

_____

_____

_____

_____

_____

_____

_____

_____

_____

_____

_____

_____

_____

_____

_____

_____

_____

_____

12

How do your fellow classmates remember you?

13

What school activities, sports, or clubs did you participate in? Were you involved in music, drama, or the school band?

14

Did you go to school dances? Did you have dates? What were they like? What songs or dances were popular?

15

Did you receive any awards or recognition
in high school?

16

What was your graduation like? What did you wear?

_____

_____

_____

_____

_____

_____

_____

_____

_____

_____

_____

_____

_____

_____

_____

_____

_____

_____

_____

_____

17

Have you attended any high school reunions? What impressed you most?

Your
Cultural History

What kind of clothing did you wear? Were there fads? How were your clothes different from clothes and hairstyles today?

2

How old were you when you got your driver's license? Did you have your own car?

_____

_____

_____

_____

_____

_____

_____

_____

_____

_____

_____

_____

_____

_____

_____

_____

_____

_____

_____

_____

3

Who most influenced your thinking
during your growing-up years? Why?

4

Did you have a mentor or friend you
admired and followed? Is there one person
who really changed the course of your life
by something that person said or did?

5

What was the name of the first boy you liked? Did you ever go on a date with him?

6

Do you remember the first time you wore makeup? Did you do it behind your parents' backs, or did they encourage it?

_____

_____

_____

_____

_____

_____

_____

_____

_____

_____

_____

_____

_____

_____

_____

_____

_____

_____

_____

_____

_____

SHARE YOUR STORIES

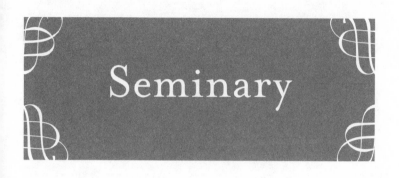

Seminary

Where did you attend seminary?

2

Which were your favorite classes or teachers?

3

What did you enjoy most about your favorite classes?

4

What special events or activities do you recall?

5

What did you feel was the most important
thing you gained from your seminary
experiences?

_____

_____

_____

_____

_____

_____

_____

_____

_____

_____

_____

_____

_____

_____

_____

_____

_____

_____

_____

_____

Early Adulthood
(18 to 25 years old)

Young
Adulthood

Describe your personality as a young adult.

2

Did you attend any school or training after high school? How many years of education have you completed?

3

Do you have any college degrees or
training certificates? From where? What
was your major or area of study?

_____

_____

_____

_____

_____

_____

_____

_____

_____

_____

_____

_____

_____

_____

_____

_____

_____

_____

4

What were your roommates like? Tell a
story about an enjoyable time you had
together.

_____

_____

_____

_____

_____

_____

_____

_____

_____

_____

_____

_____

_____

_____

_____

_____

_____

_____

_____

What important world events do you remember from this time in your life?

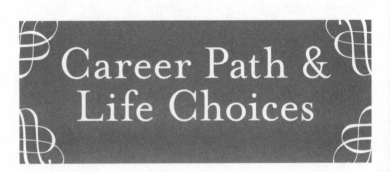

Career Path & Life Choices

1

As a child, what did you want to be when you grew up?

2

What was your first job? What kind of salary were you paid?

What kinds of jobs have you had?

4

How did you decide on the career path your life has taken?

5

What lessons about life have you learned from your career?

Military
Service

When and where did you serve, and what were your duties? Rank?

2

Were you ever injured in the line of duty?
What were the circumstances?

_____

_____

_____

_____

_____

_____

_____

_____

_____

_____

_____

_____

_____

_____

_____

_____

_____

_____

_____

_____

_____

_____

Where were you stationed?

4

What are some of the things you remember about being in the service?

_____

_____

_____

_____

_____

_____

_____

_____

_____

_____

_____

_____

_____

_____

_____

_____

_____

_____

_____

5

What are your feelings about your service to your country?

MILITARY SERVICE

Mission
Experiences

Describe the decision process you went through before you chose to go on a mission. What motivated you to go? Was your family supportive of your decision to serve?

_____
_____
_____
_____
_____
_____
_____
_____
_____
_____
_____
_____
_____
_____
_____
_____
_____
_____

2

When were you called on a mission?

3

Where did you serve? Which areas did you serve in? How long did you serve in each area?

4

Who set you apart?

5

Who were your companions?

6

What are some of the most interesting experiences from your mission?

_____

_____

_____

_____

_____

_____

_____

_____

_____

_____

_____

_____

_____

_____

_____

_____

_____

_____

_____

_____

What was the most spiritual thing that happened to you on your mission?

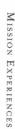

Prime Adulthood
(25 to 45 years old)

Dating, Courting, and Marriage

How old were you when you started dating?

2

Do you remember your first date? Who
was it with? What did you do?

_____

_____

_____

_____

_____

_____

_____

_____

_____

_____

_____

_____

_____

_____

_____

_____

_____

_____

_____

_____

_____

3

When, where, and how did you meet your
husband? How old were both of you?

4

Do you remember where you went on your first date with him? What was it like?

5

What attracted you to him?

6

Tell about your courtship. How long did
you know him before you got married?

_____

_____

_____

_____

_____

_____

_____

_____

_____

_____

_____

_____

_____

_____

_____

_____

_____

_____

_____

_____

7

How did he propose? How long were you engaged?

8

When and where did you get married?
Describe the wedding ceremony and who
was there.

9

What are some memories of your wedding?

10

Did you have a honeymoon? Where did you go?

_____

_____

_____

_____

_____

_____

_____

_____

_____

_____

_____

_____

_____

_____

_____

_____

_____

_____

_____

_____

11

What adjustments did you both have to make in marriage? Were there any surprises?

Did you know how to cook when you
got married? Did you have any cooking
disasters?

_____

_____

_____

_____

_____

_____

_____

_____

_____

_____

_____

_____

_____

_____

_____

_____

_____

_____

_____

13

What are some of your early marriage experiences?

14

Where was your first home as a married
couple? What other homes have you lived in?

15

Where have you most enjoyed living?
Why? Why are you living where you are
today?

_____
_____
_____
_____
_____
_____
_____
_____
_____
_____
_____
_____
_____
_____
_____
_____
_____
_____

16

How would you describe your husband
now? How long have you been married?

_____

_____

_____

_____

_____

_____

_____

_____

_____

_____

_____

_____

_____

_____

_____

_____

_____

_____

_____

_____

_____

17

What do you admire most about him? Tell
a favorite story or two about him.

18

What advice would you give to your children or grandchildren on their wedding day?

Parenthood

How did you feel when you found out
you were going to be a mother for the
first time?

2

How many children have you had? What are their names, birthdays, birthplaces?

3

Were there any unique circumstances surrounding their births?

4

Why did you give them the names you did?

_____

_____

_____

_____

_____

_____

_____

_____

_____

_____

_____

_____

_____

_____

_____

_____

_____

_____

5

What are some of the funniest moments
(things they said or did) you can
remember about your children?

6

Do you remember anything your children did when they were small that surprised or amazed you?

What are some of the blessings you have received from raising your children?

8

What did you find most rewarding about raising a family?

9

What was the most difficult thing about raising a family?

10

What advice would you give to your children about being a parent?

If you had it to do all over again, how would you change the way you raised your family?

_____
_____
_____
_____
_____
_____
_____
_____
_____
_____
_____
_____
_____
_____
_____
_____
_____
_____
_____
_____
_____
_____

Church
Affiliation
and Service

What religion did your parents and grandparents practice?

2

When were you baptized? What do you remember about the event?

3

When and where were you endowed? What
do you remember about your endowment?

_____

_____

_____

_____

_____

_____

_____

_____

_____

_____

_____

_____

_____

_____

_____

_____

_____

_____

_____

_____

4

What experiences in the Church do you treasure most?

5

Are there any insights from studying the scriptures or attending conferences you would like to pass on to your children?

6

When did you receive a testimony of the Savior?

_____

_____

_____

_____

_____

_____

_____

_____

_____

_____

_____

_____

_____

_____

_____

_____

_____

_____

What are your feelings about God?

8

As you look back over your experiences in the Church, what lessons have you learned that you would like to pass on to your posterity?

_____
_____
_____
_____
_____
_____
_____
_____
_____
_____
_____
_____
_____
_____
_____
_____
_____
_____
_____

9

Have you had any faith-promoting
experiences (receiving answers to prayers,
meeting Church leaders, and so on)?

SHARE YOUR STORIES

10

Have you had any special priesthood blessings?

11

Why do you have faith in God? How have you built your faith in God?

_____

12

What are some of your favorite scriptures,
quotes, or sayings?

_____

_____

_____

_____

_____

_____

_____

_____

_____

_____

_____

_____

_____

_____

_____

_____

_____

_____

_____

13

What is your creed for living a good life?

14

What callings have you held in the Church? With whom did you serve?

Community
Service

What community projects have you worked on?

_____

_____

_____

_____

_____

_____

_____

_____

_____

_____

_____

_____

_____

_____

_____

_____

_____

_____

2

What volunteer work have you done?

3

What spiritual lessons have you learned
from your service to others?

_____

_____

_____

_____

_____

_____

_____

_____

_____

_____

_____

_____

_____

_____

_____

_____

_____

_____

Middle Adult Years
(45 to 60 years old)

Loss of
Loved Ones

When and where did your parents die?

2

What do you remember about the death
of your parents and your thoughts and
feelings at the time?

_____

_____

_____

_____

_____

_____

_____

_____

_____

_____

_____

_____

_____

_____

_____

_____

_____

_____

Did you know your grandparents or great-grandparents? What do you remember about them and their lives?

_____

_____

_____

_____

_____

_____

_____

_____

_____

_____

_____

_____

_____

_____

_____

_____

_____

4

Do you remember hearing your
grandparents or great-grandparents
describe anything about their lives?

_____

_____

_____

_____

_____

_____

_____

_____

_____

_____

_____

_____

_____

_____

_____

_____

_____

_____

5

Did your grandparents or great-grandparents relate important world events they experienced?

6

Are there any family heirlooms that have been passed from one generation to another?

_____

_____

_____

_____

_____

_____

_____

_____

_____

_____

_____

_____

_____

_____

_____

_____

_____

_____

When, where, and how did your husband die? Where is he buried?

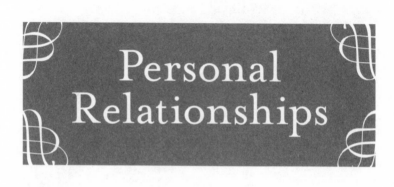

Personal Relationships

1

Which of your good friends have you known the longest?

_____

_____

_____

_____

_____

_____

_____

_____

_____

_____

_____

_____

_____

_____

_____

_____

_____

_____

2

What do you admire
most about that person?

3

What memories do you have about your experiences together?

_____

_____

_____

_____

_____

_____

_____

_____

_____

_____

_____

_____

_____

_____

_____

_____

_____

_____

_____

_____

4

Has anyone ever saved your life? Who?
What were the circumstances?

Later Adulthood
(65 to present)

Personal
Reflections

1

What do you consider to be the most important historical event of your lifetime? What do you recall about it? Where were you when it occurred?

2

What were some other important historical events of your lifetime? What do you recall about them? Where were you when they occurred?

...(continued)

3

What wars have been fought during your lifetime?

4

What impact did those wars
have on your life? Did you support
or oppose those wars?

_____

_____

_____

_____

_____

_____

_____

_____

_____

_____

_____

_____

_____

_____

_____

_____

_____

5

What are the most important inventions
or discoveries made during your lifetime?

6

How would you describe yourself politically? Why?

Which public leaders have you admired the most? Why?

8

As you see it, what are the biggest problems facing our nation, and how do you think they can be solved?

_____

_____

_____

_____

_____

_____

_____

_____

_____

_____

_____

_____

_____

_____

_____

_____

_____

_____

9

What activities have you especially enjoyed as an adult?

10

Is there anything you have always wanted to do but haven't done yet?

11

Have you received any memorable letters
you would like to have your children and
grandchildren read?

_____

_____

_____

_____

_____

_____

_____

_____

_____

_____

_____

_____

_____

_____

_____

_____

_____

_____

_____

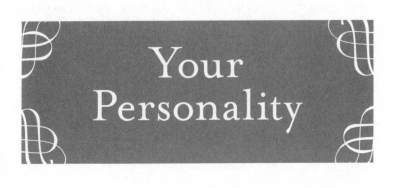

Your Personality

What were the most difficult choices you
ever had to make? How do you feel about
the results of your decisions?

_____

_____

_____

_____

_____

_____

_____

_____

_____

_____

_____

_____

_____

_____

_____

_____

_____

_____

_____

_____

_____

SHARE YOUR STORIES

If you could change something about yourself, what would it be?

3

What was the scariest or most stressful thing
that ever happened to you? What helped you
get through it?

4

Do you play any musical instruments?

5

What is your favorite type of music?

6

Do you consider yourself to be creative or artistic?

_____

_____

_____

_____

_____

_____

_____

_____

_____

_____

_____

_____

_____

_____

_____

_____

_____

_____

7

What unique talents or skills have you developed?

8

What are your hobbies? Do you have any collections (stamps, coins, rocks, embroidery)?

_____

_____

_____

_____

_____

_____

_____

_____

_____

_____

_____

_____

_____

_____

_____

_____

9

What are your favorite movies?

10

How would you describe your sense of humor?

11

What are the funniest practical jokes you ever
played on someone or had played on you?

12

What are some of your favorite books?

13

How do you feel about the future?
What advice for the future
would you give your posterity?

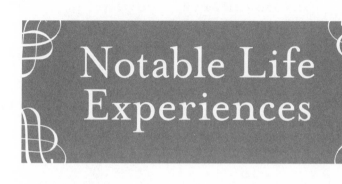

Notable Life Experiences

Have you ever received any special awards
or recognition in your life?
What were they?

_____

_____

_____

_____

_____

_____

_____

_____

_____

_____

_____

_____

_____

_____

_____

_____

_____

_____

_____

2

Have you ever met any famous people? Describe what happened.

3

Can you describe a time and place when
you remember feeling happy to be alive?
Where were you and what were you doing?

_____

_____

_____

_____

_____

_____

_____

_____

_____

_____

_____

_____

_____

_____

_____

_____

_____

_____

4

What was your favorite vacation?

5

How many states have you been in?
List them.

6

How many countries have you been in?
List them.

_____

_____

_____

_____

_____

_____

_____

_____

_____

_____

_____

_____

_____

_____

_____

_____

_____

_____

_____

7

What was the longest trip you've ever taken? Who were you with, and where did you travel?

8

What has been your the favorite place to visit? What was it like?

9

Have you ever seen or been in a natural
disaster? What kind? Where?

_____

_____

_____

_____

_____

_____

_____

_____

_____

_____

_____

_____

_____

_____

_____

_____

_____

_____

_____

_____

_____

10

Have you ever suffered any serious illness
or injury? Describe what happened and
how you recovered.

_____

_____

_____

_____

_____

_____

_____

_____

_____

_____

_____

_____

_____

_____

_____

_____

_____

NOTES

NOTES

NOTES

NOTES

NOTES

NOTES

NOTES

NOTES

Mother:

0 26575 79584 4

Grandma:

0 26575 79606 3